POLLINATORS ARE OUR FRI

Thank You, Bugs!

DAWN PAPE

Thank You, Bugs!

DAWN PAPE

To my Mason and Maxwell . . . and every beloved other child too.

GOOD GREEN LIFE
— publishing —

P.O. Box 74
Circle Pines, MN 55014-1793

Photos were taken by the author with these exceptions:
Laura Monahan: boy on bridge on p. 4 and 38; boy with arms stretched on p. 36; boys hugging on p. 37
Shutterstock: apples, butterfly, bee on cover; butterfly on p. 5 and 35; deer ticks on p. 6; centipedes on p. 8;
mosquitoes on p. 10; cherries on p. 26-27; berries on p. 29 and 33; cucumber on p. 30-31;
food, butterflies, bees on p. 44-45
Heather Holm: mason bee on flower p. 42
Dave Hunter: mason bee with pollen p. 43

January 14, 2016
ISBN: 978-0-9971131-0-5
Keywords: bees, bugs, insects, wild bees, beneficial insects, pollination, pollinators,
facial expressions, non-verbal cues, emotions

PRINTED IN THE UNITED STATES OF AMERICA

Hi, I'm Mason.
I have a question for you.

Do you like bugs?

It's true.
Some bugs *are*
SCARY!

Deer ticks

How do you look when you're scared?

Some bugs look kind of

HAIRY.

Centipedes

This is my "that's yucky" face.
What does your "yucky" face look like?

Some bugs
BITE...

Mosquitoes

OUCH!

...and keep me up at night!

SCRATCH, SCRATCH, SCRATCH!

DARN MOSQUITOES!

But even though some bugs truly *are* a hairy, scary bother, lots of bugs are good!

And if you don't like them,

you should!

It's just that
insects help make
a <u>lot</u> of the food we eat—

like apples...

and cherries...

and so many types of berries...

even cucumbers
and squash...

OH MY GOSH!

Thank you!

THANK YOU!

Shukrān (Arabic)

Grazie! (Italian)

Salamat po! (Tagalog)

Kamsahamnida! (Korean)

Xièxiè (Mandarin Chinese)

Ua tsaug! (Hmong)

Thank you, little bugs!

Xin cảm ơn (Vietnamese)

¡Gracias! (Spanish)

Danke! (German)

Merci! (French)

спасибо (Russian)

In how many languages can you say thank you?

If we could, we'd give you
GREAT BIG...

How far can you stretch out your arms?

HUGS!

Since you can't hug a bug,
how about hugging the person next to you?

Now do you like bugs?

Check out
additional pre-school
discussion and lessons about
pollination on the following pages!

Yes, I guess I do.
But I've been wondering about something too.

How do insects help make the food we eat?

It may sound a little crazy,
but those pollinating insects sure aren't lazy.

They drink flower nectar for hours and hours
when they visit lots and lots of flowers.

As insects like bees, butterflies, and moths drink
"flower juice" called nectar, dust-like pollen sticks to
their legs and bodies, you see,
and as they visit the next flower, some of the pollen falls
off and they accidentally made a pollen delivery!

This *magical* pollen delivery
is just exactly what the plants need
to turn their flowers into seeds.

Then with a little rain and sunshine
the seeds grow into food so we can dine!

IF YOUR FIRST REACTION IS TO KILL BUGS, you're not alone. But I urge you to put down the bottle of insecticide and step away before you do anything you might regret later. Let's remind ourselves that insects do more good in the world than bad, and few insects need to be controlled.

Many insects—such as bees, butterflies, lacewings, wasps, tachinid flies, and beetles—pollinate our food. Perhaps we should be thanking pollinators at each meal, since about every third bite of food is thanks to a pollinators. Besides fruits and vegetables, remember coffee, chocolate, vanilla and even meat and dairy products—since cows eat alfalfa. The value of good nutrition is pretty tough to quantify, but fruits, vegetables and nut crops alone are worth around 20 billion dollars.

Of course, insects also provide other products such as cotton, silk, lac (ingredient in floor and shoe polishes, insulators, various sealants, printing inks, and varnish), beeswax (base for ointments, polishes, candle making, lotions, creams, and lipsticks) as well as dyes. To boot, fruit flies have long been used in genetic studies.

It is true that certain invasive species warrant "chemical warfare" (pesticides), however, this is the exception, not the rule. Keep in mind, once a broad-spectrum insecticide is used, the beneficial insects, like dragonflies and ladybugs that provide a pest removal service, are killed too. Once the good guys are gone, little can stop attacks by the bad guys except using more pesticides. This is a dangerous and vicious cycle. Beneficial insects will also only lay eggs if pests are present in high enough numbers to feed their young. This is another reason not to get hasty with the pesticides. If we kill all the bad guys, the good guys won't reproduce.

It is important to be able to identify the bug as friend, foe, or just a nuisance before taking any action. There are resources on the following pages to help you identify bugs.

Extension Activities

ACT IT OUT!

Have kids be busy little insects and drink nectar (aka juice) from pretend flowers as they sit in a pile of pollen (e.g. felt scraps, cotton balls or dried leaves...). When the kids "fly" to the next flower, see how much "pollen" they accidentally delivered.

DO BUGS DO MORE GOOD OR BAD IN THE WORLD?

Ask the students if they think insects do more good in the world or more harm. You may want to note the "before" hands and "after" hands after reading the book to see if the book influenced their opinions.

Next, ask the students what words come to mind when they think about insects. As they come up with ideas, show the students the corresponding picture (printed off from www.lawnchairgardener.com). Have two clear containers. Put a bead (or similar object) in the appropriate "positive" or "negative" container for each idea. If the kids come up with ideas not included on the pictures, make a drawing to represent that on a new sheet of paper and add it to the pile. If the kids come up with different words for the same concept, remind them that is similar to a picture already shown, (e.g. "icky," "gross," "scary," etc.) Since pollination is so valuable for our survival, put many beads in the container. At the end, look at the containers to see if insects are "more good" or "more bad."

Please note, you may have to "stack the deck" because it seems natural for people to have an aversion to insects, but the point of this lesson is to show that insects do, indeed, do more good in the world than bad and they are extremely valuable to our daily eating.

RESOURCES TO HELP IDENTIFY INSECTS

Center for Invasive Species and Ecosystem Health
(bugwood.org)

Good Bug Bad Bug: Who's Who, What They Do, and How to Manage Them Organically *(All You Need to Know about the Insects in Your Garden)*, by Jessica Walliser.

Minnesota Department of Agriculture
(www.mda.state.mn.us/plants/pestmanagement/invasivesunit.aspx)

National Invasive Species Council
(http://www.invasivespecies.gov)

University of Minnesota Extension Service
"What's wrong with my plant?"and "What insect is this?" (extension.umn.edu/garden)
Also check your state's local extension office

USGS Nonindigenous Aquatic Species
(http://nas.er.usgs.gov)

EXTENSION ACTIVITIES AND LESSONS FOR CHILDREN

Garden at School (gardenatschool.wordpress.com)
Tips for engaging kids with gardening activities, pollination games, seed dispersal lessons, parts of plants, scavenger hunts, composting and more...

Lawn Chair Gardener (lawnchairgardener.com)
PreK garden curriculum, book lists, songs and more

Pollinator Partnership (pollinator.org/education.htm)
PreK-12 curriculum, lesson plans, extension ideas, background information for the teacher, educational tools, activities, contests, food, fun, facts, talking points, PowerPoint presentations and links.

U.S. Department of Agriculture (usda.gov/wps/portal/usda/usdahome?navid=FOR_KIDS)
Lessons on nutrition, gardening, conservation, insects, soil, etc.

CPSIA information can be obtained
at www.ICGtesting.com
Printed in the USA
BVHW021659040522
636120BV00004B/60

9 780997 113105